AMERICAN PI

POETIC IMPLOSION

$$\pi$$

J. CHRISTIAN

AuthorHouse™
1663 Liberty Drive
Bloomington, IN 47403
www.authorhouse.com
Phone: 833-262-8899

Because of the dynamic nature of the Internet, any web addresses or links contained in this book may have changed since publication and may no longer be valid. The views expressed in this work are solely those of the author and do not necessarily reflect the views of the publisher, and the publisher hereby disclaims any responsibility for them.

Any people depicted in stock imagery provided by Getty Images are models, and such images are being used for illustrative purposes only.
Certain stock imagery © Getty Images.

This book is printed on acid-free paper.

ISBN: 978-1-6655-3939-5 (sc)
ISBN: 978-1-6655-3940-1 (e)

Print information available on the last page.

Published by AuthorHouse 11/17/2021

authorHOUSE®

AMERICAN PI

POETIC IMPLOSION

PRESENT

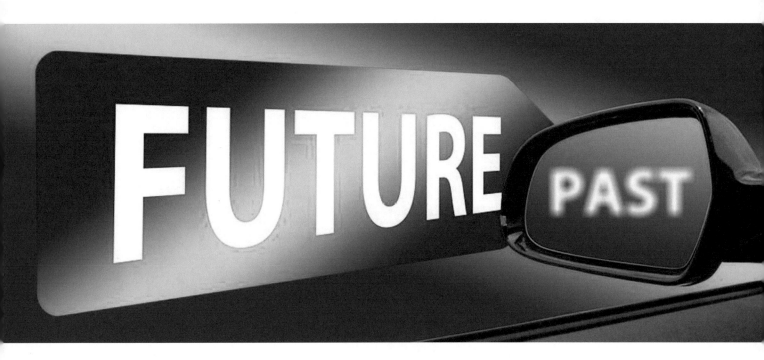

SAY CHEESE!

Back and forths do not occur

in isolation.

U.S. sneezes, England cheeks in

"God bless you!"

Power on cell can easily tell
We are on camera
We are global
Leading social linkage to...

Little Joey in Kentucky

sharing snapchats

of the new pet

bearded dragon

he named Ace

With a kid in Cameroon hoping
to know one day soon
Why a lizard lives in such
a fancy place.
(and indoors!)

SIDE VIEW MYHRE

People in this country
are closer than they appear

Perception, media receptions
have not made it clear

Our history
Our unions
Show

America Endures

We hold our nation
Under God.

Under A Rest

Assured.

V.O.T.E

When we go...

V. oice

O. ur

T. houghts

E. lectorally

It's then and how we are heard.

Put your fingerprint on history.
Is Electorally even a word?

HOW WE

How we love our country
is expressed in different ways

Some choose to serve
in uniform
For freedom we display

Some protest for
wanting most
the best
for all of us

While others pray
in silence
that we all
can learn to trust

One another more.
Pledge Allegiance and
Stand tall

With liberty and justice
for us all!

EYES RHYME

We have
Possessions
People
Property

Ideas
Borrowed
Never owned

Seeds stolen
Snatched away
Then planted

Elsewhere

Reaping
Wrath
as sown!

BLAME

Blame present day
for History
Implicit
Bias defined

Blame Blacks for
the fear of dark
Blame policemen
For crime

Blame yellow lights
for turning red
Because you were
Short on time

Blame Whites
All Whites
Even the poor
For privilege design

Choosing to look
the other way from
Injustice galore

We simply can not
do that
Anymore

FSBO

Whoever pays for you
Owns you

Buyer is the one
Who owns

Owners finance
The song
The dance

Determine who
Can sing along

Payers dictate rights to powers

Given them by debts they are owed

Dictaters
decide the hours,
minutes,
milliseconds
Sold!

Empowered Loaners
Indebted moaners
Symbiotic
Servant pair

Leasing land for
Souls from owners
Forever floating
Everywhere

HEAR YE!

In accordance with the
One drop rule and 3/5th Declaration,
We are Constituted now
all 5/5th
multi-colored nation.

Standing.
Kneeling.
Allegiant.
Healing.

Natives and 'other from'.

Under God
One nation
Freedom.
Liberty.

Justice
for some.

YOU S. A.?

The question is

Which one are you?

a Suspect

or Accuser?

You, Knighted
state
of fate demised?

Or lying tongue

Abuser?

One who perched

Berating

Creates absent

Evidence?

Or cautious
and awaiting
Mayhem
Flung over the fence?

So, which…

Suspect? Accuser?

Devising harm

In others minds

All can see

Cast as amusers

Then go take your
Place in line.

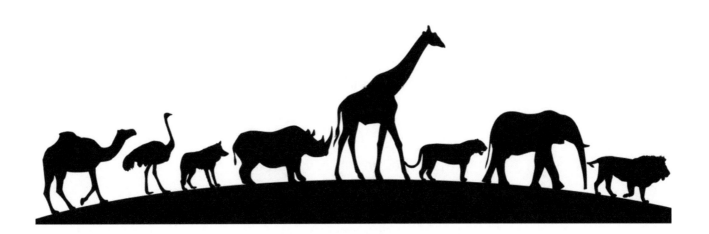

HEAR YE CLEARLY

If we cannot pull Peace off
together
We will see our nation slowly
pulled apart

Read the U.S. Constitution
Declaration of Independence
Bill of Rights then
Remember in the start

Of USA, we bickered
Who would lead us
What to follow,
When would swallow,
Why ignore

We weren't friends though in the end we came together
We all knew what causes we were fighting for

Freedom from Oppression
Freedom for Due Justice
An end to unfair tyranny
And strife

Freedom to express
And chance to be the best
For religion, to protect ourselves
For life

We mostly got it right the 1st time.
Good guys - us
Bad guys - them
So far away

Now we are still together
Let's take an oath again no matter
What the circumstance
We'll vow keep it this way

RECON TWO POINT- OH!

R. econstruct

E. quality.

C. onstitution

O. n the line.

N. ew views

S. tating clearly

T. ogether we must

R. edefine.

U. nderstanding the

C. ivility

T. akes priority

I. n all

O. r very things we stand for

N. ow will fall!

R.I.P.

Rest in peril, weapons drawn to erase binding ties of this
nation

The unraveling hatred pulling apart the seams holding duration

For centuries so taut divising
the divisions became blurred

Covered up by the dust of scampering footsteps.
Flags unfurled.

Across state lines shifting timelines to and fro.
and Bros.

Rest in praise the souls
of warriors inside
to send outside their rote

Their own lives above the blurred lines buried beneath the tools wit dared

use armaments against Almighty weapons.
All beware

No humor thinking hate
So close to victory
Before warnings

R.est I.n P.rayer.

GOAT

Over and over the greatest of all time performances

Take place unceremoniously
no grandstands

Earthbound impact messages
recollection

The son came down to us once
as a man

Who performed life miracles
lauded "lo behold!"

Though not applauded and
no bronze, silver, or gold

EXHIBITS

I wish I could depart from here
and climb inside myself

Operate my thoughts
and actions from in there

It would not matter
if I was pretty
Pretty ugly

Fat or thin

Or the color
Or the texture
Of my hair

My exhibits have such impact
Oft avoided; can ensnare
All your senses
Your decision not to care.

FELL

If a tree falls

In the Forest

And no one hears

Is there a sound?

If a heart breaks

In the Family

And no one cares

Will it be found…

Ever?
Forever?

BEFORE NOW

Someone posed the question,

"Do you remember
who you were before
the world got to you?"

(silent recollection)

Try hard to remember.
Life once pure and
Simple. True.

Before you were too…

Had too little…

Wore too much…

Were the wrong…

Did those things…

Heard that.

Felt that.

Sang your mantra songs?

Had others
In allegiance
Sing along.

THIS IS PRIVATE

How can we decide

to showcase

our everything

While begging

same observers

to not dare

look?

Have deep secrets very personal

Held privately inside

Except in published pages of a book?

BOTHERED BY B's

Great great grandpa
Hated B's
He heard all they do is sting

Though perception was
Ungrounded
Ones he saw hurt not a thing

He would SWAT them. Hard.
Deliberate.
Made example of the hive

They need clear out
Expeditiously
If want to stay alive

B's all knew from experience
Men with swatters
Like to splat

So anticipated
Angry Actions
From all men like that

Great Grandpas are bothered by B's
B's are bothered by those men.

(c'mon let's face this
no one is racist
just bothered by
the skin)

Instead....

Think, Honey,
Pollination
Flowers
Jubilation
Joys!

Not the stinging
Buzzing
Bringing
Thoughts of Fear
To Girls and
Boys

God created 'Thems'
and 'Us's'

For sweet harmony in songs

For Buzzing Syncopated

U.S.All to get along!

CRITICS

Given a choice between the way
Things turn out be
With the best efforts
The best interests
Depth of sincerity

God given talents
Giving balance to
What naysayers would think

Divine describe
Exactly what you see.
Succinct

Some will like it
Some will not

Giving everything
You got

To share stories
And His glory

Abhor

Care less
What critics
Think
Forevermore.

NO RIGHT TO EDUCATION

Brown v. new brown generation

New musicians misspelling same songs,

Educashun

Educasion

EDUCATION

is a

Privilige

Privalage

Priveledge

Privileged **PRIVILEGE**

Not Right; some try

With disabled deny

How could this ever go wrung?

TRACTORS

Tractors are vital vehicles

To aide at harvest time

Controlled by motors
Many Motivated

Farmers in Combines

Let's not take them for granted

Yes, they are big
They are not dumb

At least right now
They know

Where they are going.
Where they're from.

They are going
to and 'fro

To their fields
to get
Work done

THUMBS UP

Praise the
Possibilities
We can all be
Friends

Caring
Kindness
(true)
Color
Blindness

Are what matter
In the end

Warmth has same
Hues, Temperatures
Hugs resonated from

Smiling friends.
Hyperextend
Hale
Upward pointed thumbs

TEAM CAPTAIN

Here's the best part
Picking sides
Choose the team Captains first

The most vocal
Deemed the leader of the pack

Race and age
Insignificant
Power and passion most essential
Cannot lack...

The appearance as the strongest

With a catchy mantra

Songstress to abide

Beaming and gleaming
with
Clear confidence

and pride.

(except inside)

LET'S TALK

I don't know how to talk to you
I do know what to say
I have unsown seeds for fertile soil
I want to spread your way

I long to make
Connections
Together forward
We should step

Please see my heart
So we can start
Our country needs the help

To heal our pain,
Unite again
before we fall apart

I don't know how to talk to you
I know this is a start

CONNECTIONS

When you break connect i o n s

You l o
        s
          E

            P

        O

          W

            e

          r

AWAKE

Mere fact you use

"I have a Dream"

To make a point with

Me

Gives credence to those

Who opine

It's color that you see

Color used

to make the point

not using it

Falls Flat

Winning the case

We have moved

So far beyond

THAT

SINCE US 2020

Far too many here to hide us
Too blatant.
Look the other way.

Far too grounded
To dig; toss aside
The truth you learned today.

Fact: our genes and your genes
Are as one.
Multiplied.

DNA bound
Biologically
Multi Mixed Inside.

Any who choose to hate us,
ostracize or berate us,
Asinine.
Asking all to cease,

Celebrate who we are
Grounded Genetically
Embodying personas of Peace

We are same uniquely different
in numbers
high and strong.

In divine deference
Here We Belong

VOLUME

We can hear you loud and clear now.
(Why so loudly?)

Why right here?

And now, this moment,
Point in time?

We can hear you
with the volume down

Seeing is louder than the sound

Nothing of your presence is sublime.

No crosses for the other seems
the best and only way to be.

So you can have your place
and I have mine.

Why can't we just go separate ways?

Be kind?

K.I.S.S.

Keep it simple Senators,

House - a common ground.

The world is watching,

Waiting, judging

How this all goes down.

Win. It is over.

Under. Stand.

Under same

Flag.

Still

U. S.

A

U.nified S.tate

Stay

United.

We will!

IGNORE-RANTS

(wine glass shape*)

Rantaholics find it impossible not to
pause for cause or stop and take a sip
of rant poison just because like this one
from someone who goes on and on about
something and some thing for so long the
audience gets lost in lyrics then they too
find themselves sipping words of a song
then find themselves tapping along
touching temples first
thinking then rapping
wrapping around
rants repeating
words without
clarity because
clarity rhymes
with little and
rants require
'real bigness'
to remain
credible
though
credible
and credibility
also rhyme with little so has no place in
ignorance so ignore rants and move along.

3.14159 TIME

Three more people try to find

Point of living while no

One there

Four

Ones who

Five sans five plus

Nine-t plus 10 percent

Really truly would not dare

if someone goes around and cares

Gives a hand.
It is difficult to explain
or understand

<u>PI</u>

On and on

Encircling

Calculating

Never Ends

Multiples to

Circle Back

Tether Hope
'round
God and Friends

Rings of Love

Surround our Country

Discorders should all join hands

Interlock or unintentionally

lessen our beloved land

PAST

THIS TOO

Disco
Bell bottom pants
Corded phones
Book burning rants

Silent Movies
Segregated Schools
Pagers
Exclusion Rules

Roaring 20's
Platform Shoes
Groovy
Paper only news

Dinosaurs
Leaded Gas
Leisure Suits
Typing Class

Hatred - yes, one day this too
shall pass

NEW NEW SOUTH

Grady of The New South cries out
"now it is your turn!"

This place is trying to slip apart
go show them what you learned

That left and right and
north and south
are far more than directions

And we can't run a whole country
divided into sections

By now we should face forward
not backwards have to look

for resolution lessons
chronicled in history books.

The U.S. is us and us U.S. in the U.S.A.
Fifty parts together have to operate that way

And colors? Do they matter?
You best believe they do.

Our banners fly in bright
Red, White and Blue

All colors? Yes, they matter!
You best believe they do.

Aside flag flying Higher -
Red, White, Blue

SALLY SAT

Sally sat at the table

After all, she cooked

The food

Did the
Dishes

Dirty laundry
Then in darkness

Did him good

Fed his children

Then their children

Helped to Feign
a happy life

As he sat
digesting dinner
at the table with his wife

SEEDS

yOur seeds yOur seeds yOur seeds
fertilized
Cotton-picking soil

Watered by the tears cried
coercive
Farming fainting toil

The blood the blood our blood
Was flowing
Intered coarse to be

Sweat. Saturated soaked in
Science.
Proof.

Positive.

You.are.Me.

ACCOUNTABILITY

Since you and I have never met

Why oh why should I regret

what my ancestors may have done
(mine were not the only ones)

...to yours?

Why the accountability

for things never done by me?

Your voices, vigilance so loud

Ignores...

Purpose and platforms are
Too proud.
Boisterous volume is way too loud.

Quietly, please. Lower your tone.

Let's just let bygones be gone.

Bye; gone.

PURELY SCIENTIFIC

Challenge all
Who are grounded in hatred

Ethnic purity
Assured they are just

In declaration
Homogenous stated

DNA confirm
In God and science Trust

Dare:

Share the findings with all of us.

DeHUMAN CAPITAL

Millions and millions
Worked for free
Sang reparation songs

Sharecropped for pay to do the job that was already done

Nope. Go away. Move over say
no reminder whence from.

We can negotiate or power prove
our ropes and our guns

It fear-made sense to pay more cents; train those who immigrate.

In different tongues paid multiples of reparations rate.

IMPRESSION

We love riches
Will kill for
Them are not
As smart.
As think...

Skene is powerful
Donned daggers.
Weapons drawn
In pictures.
Drink...

Whine of watters
Poured in oceans
Claimed as
Chattel;
Owned. Command.

Scenes as deemed
Manifestation
All ours.
Wonders, World and
Land.

EMANCIPATE-SHUN

Go if you must
In God go trust
Imports will compensate.

In different tongues
Paid multiples of
Reparations rate.

Now free to roam
about in doubt
aimlessly
Seeking land

And family, identity,
Way to be
A man

Ample opportunity
to work this
land for free

Alongside others
Elsewhere from
Paid with your dignity

OUR SEEDS

Our seeds our seeds your seeds
provided
For cotton-picking soil

Watered by reigned workers
guiding
Grounding planter toil

The blood their blood our Blood
Was flowing
Entered course so fine

Sweat. Sweet plantated
saturated
Scientific.
Proof.

I own.

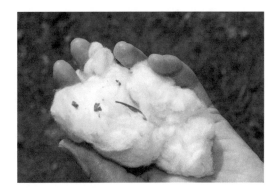

you.
are.mIne.

O'IRONY

Millions and millions
Worked for free
Sang reparation songs

The Drummer beat
prevenely ceased
(plantation gigs were wrong)

'Lo listeners oblige
Deride
'Unreasonable demands'

For pay, for life, for legal
Wife
For rights as 5/5ths man.

"No! Work must be done.
Now! We have guns!
And plenty seeds to sow

Emancipate post harvest dates!
Post picking plants we grow.

Don't go!"

NOT EMPTY HANDED

Just because you are holding nothing

Does not mean you are

Empty handed.

You are…

Full hearted

Breathing

Thinking

On your own.

A child of God

Has riches -

Much!

Full of faith

With Fathers

Touch

A place to be where

He can always call you

Home.

Shout!

We are never

empty handed

Children of Holy Father:
Branded

Not without

RESUSCITATION

Sometimes,

I can't breathe

So I have to

grab a Pen

To

Exhale

CHOSEN OUTFITS

The group of us decided before training even began,

That right was right, not Black or White.

Good guys should always win.

Most of us still know the difference.

For all of us, there're judgment calls.

It hurts when bad guys get away

And that the good ones sometimes fall.

We promise. Promise. Promise.

No one signed up to heed a call

other than protect and serve,

protect and serve you

One and all.

<u>R.I.P.</u>

May they rest in peace:
tools used
dare try chisel away the binding ties of this nation

Unraveling hatred pulls apart seams binding duration
For centuries so taut divisions betwixt thee are blurred
Covered by dust of scampered footsteps. Flags so oft unfurl.
Across states lines Shifting timelines in travel to and fro
Bros
Rest in praise ye staved inside to send out battle rote
Message concisely crafted then with inspiration shared
For all mankind for all men,
Kind all over everywhere (hate too close to victory!)
creators authored mocking notes of weaponry wit dare
Against Almighty victor peace defeats
Hate R.ests I.n P.rayer"

ON BEHALF OF

Your

Second place
Former face
Lesser thans
Fully manned

Wannabes
Once envied
Trying to's
Maker of shoes

Border bros
Watchers, so
Seeing sharing
To reveal

You showed all your a-kill-eez

kneel

KNICKNAMES

It is amaaazing how many
New Afr-any
waaays
Venues
Avenues and circumstances

Have been deriiived
to call us
That phat
Boiii
Knowbodies beneath
Dances

Deep.
Less syllables
Bro
Less Numbers tho
Looks 13% Bigger

Them.

Those POC
Dem-
Leaners aksing....

Wait!

Did you just call me knicker?

NO PRESSURE

Just the world.
Only
The universe

Insists the scribes
Imbibe

Dalliance
And dance around
over then
through.

Aside

The murk of hatred
Hurt and
Heartfelt horror

Dry eyed
Whetted
By feigned indifference

Searching for real.
Life.
With fake fingers
Trying to grasp
A pen and then

Enunciate.
And articulate .

"A body
gesticulating..."

58

Dictating the story
Dateline.
With a countdown
Of breaths

"Under pressure
Under foot..."

(soon underground)

And so the scribe
Must describe

Chronicle crisis
And remove self
From the story

For the glory
Of the "bye" lines
By the deadline.

Then go hide.

HOW TO NOW

I don't how to now

Somehow

I do not know

How to now

I can do then

Repeat again

Then fast forward

Allow

I can rear view mirror
well project
The future qualms

But now, right now
Cannot exist

So I remain
forearmed

Present
does not feel
like a gift

Still tired from
Before

Awaiting the next
Crisis

Sitting just outside
the door

Arms up?!

They never have been
Down

Dark past with
Future clouds

The past so dredged
In misery

It tramples on
The now.

SAME SAME

This is ironic
There is no way to tell the good guys
from the bad ones

The right ones from the wrongs
or to choose sides

Ask a good one who the bad one is
Its someone who just yesterday
Sat right beside at local tavern dive

They shared encounter, cheered
The Giants,
Never, not once, mentioned a riot.

Both got tipsy tall
departed newfound kin

Then in the streets next day
Forgot where they had been.

As friends.

We can not have a civil war again!

FUTURE

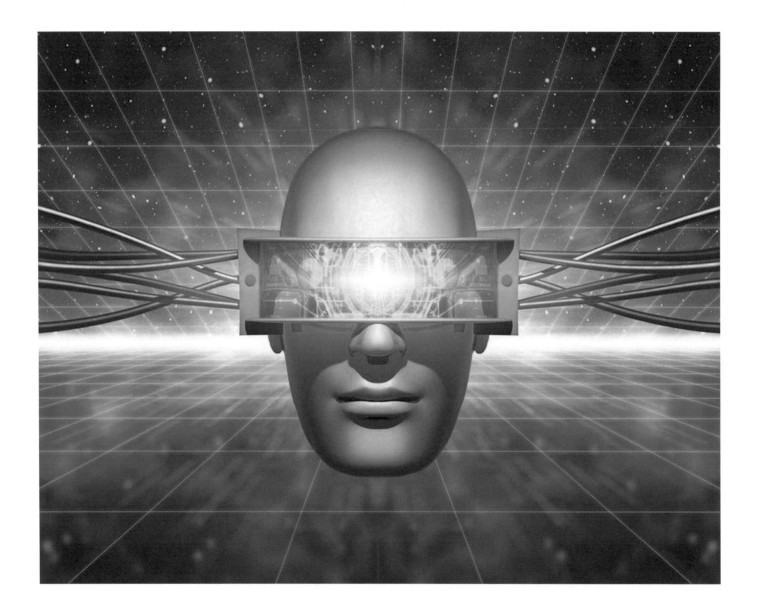

AI

Intelligence: Artificial.

Based on geographics
socio-logic
economics
derma-toxics
Poli-ticking
Voting booths

Home prices, Privileges
Pure Perky-ness
Villages
We choose to call - the truths.

Mask confusion angst amongst
Betwixt Between Belong
V-cinnated Incubated
Or not

Or forego all of these issues
Microchips instead of tissues
Artificial Intelligence
Robots

SMART SHOTS

Mr. President,
your Honor,
We need you
to take this case

It's for our children

And our country

And, with others,

To save face.

Sir, the whole world
Looks to us now.
We have set
the precedent

That our Courage

And our Valor,

our disdain,

All represent.

As a model for the others.
Let's show them
the way it's done.
1st Make a Right to Education.
2nd Build a smarter gun.

Let the world know that

Our borders

Are protected

Let's project.

'Educated regulated'
Smart militias
All
RESPECT!

DROP YOUR WEAPONS

Keep your rounds but drop your weapons. Keep your fire, pour out the fuel.

Your cannon balls are cute and all

Bandoliers look good on you.

Magazines on coffee tables

Make more sense than stuffed in guns.

All can see them there and keep them.

There.

There is...

No damage done.

ONE DAY

One day

correct will not be political

Right

Will be one direction

Left

Will be the other way

They will join at intersections

Children will all be childish

Distinguishable

From adults

Resolution will most matter

Not shaming those at fault

Worth will not be determined

By sight, only by deed

Fair honest ways

Will be conveyed

One day

One day

One day

I say

Can we please?

ACHILLES

We have shown our

Achilles Heel.

Fully Masked Face to Face

We have shown our

A-kill-ease.

HEAL.

RACE.

KIKI'S GATE

This one's for
Kiki Flack
Who always had
too much to say.

When the teacher tried
to hold her back, said
"No ma'am...
I don't play!

Refrain from
Relegation
To remedial
Because

Implicit bias
Leads you there.
Though, in the past,
It was...

OK to subvert
Intellect
To the effect-
Subdue

Ambition borne
Of retrospect
From my ancestors
Who...

Were Mocked
and
Marginalized by
People just like you."

Not anymore!

No longer.
The world's
Being rearranged.

Let's RIGHTly
Provide
Education.
Constitution;
Change

(-J-)

Knowledge
is
power!

FIVE

I think in Iambic pentameter

The reason not clearly known why

Thoughts flow in five beats

Rhythm is replete

Teacher said this was a lie.

COREd

English is our spoken tongue

Science explains what was done

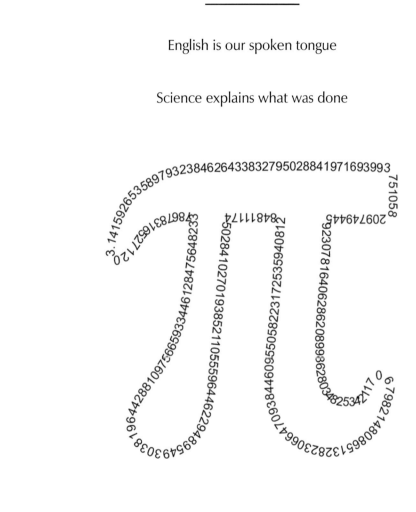

Math adds it all up in summation

Social Science gives narrations

POTHOLES

Where you choose to stand

does matter

Sitting down makes puddles splat

Jumping over turns into a game

We have had enough of that

Driving through simply disperses

Looking away has gotten old

Finally address the problems

Educate.

Fill in the holes.

QUALS

Uneducated regulated
Bare arms bearing arms

Shoot
Smart
Sharp militia

Always Right
Causing alarm

To hunt for sport
To cut life short

Recoil React Re-run

Militia; educate them
All
The 2nd right's begun

CHAIN LETTER

When asking us to
break the chains
Be mindful what
You are bearing

Was placed there by
Ancestral ghosts
Into whose face
You are staring

Sins of the fathers
Severed chances
Of advancing
Past the stares

Through the judgment
Judging worth less.
Bound to bottom
Everywhere

Ghosts chain mysteries
Blurred out history
Always changing. Always...
Shifting rounds.

Sssh!
We don't speak of that
Sssh!
Some parts must live in cracks
(not come aground)

Yes, you must wear
You must bear them
Outside Inside
Sustain

Yes, freeing
clippers are in hands
Comfort from your
Restraint

Opportunity, Equal access, Social Justice,
Higher chance,

Off you: Frees you
Though
Then we'd see you
Wandering onto the land

Ample though
It may be.
We need you to
Understand.

The fear your chains
Clanging brings
The rust;
it bears our names

Branded on it
You can not forget
We will never
be the same

Together
Rubs Entitlements
will Mix
our blood to one

Spread the wealth
Everywhere
For generations,
Son.

Our eyes too tear
When hymns we hear
With the clanging in your
Songs

We've just determined
That its best
you keep them
On

WHY'ERS

Why anyone ever
does anything
Angrily
does not ever make sense.

Why not turn eye blind

Look the other way

Find

Alternate answers

Perchance?

Yes, those things did happen
(ample evidence)
Though only
'good people'
around.

Why cause commotion

Stir up your emotion

Why not just please

Bring your voice

Down?

Besides you won't get through
Why'ers disbelief
If we decide
Nothing is there.

Your something

as solo

Is why'ers relief.

No witness so

No one else cares.

SOCIAL CONSTRUCT

It's not that we don't want you here

We just don't want to see you

Or talk to you

Or walk with you

And certainly not free you

From the burden of oppression

Or the onset of depression

That ensues

Ostracizing is much easier

We've worked too hard to be here

To not work hard

To not see you here too

HIGHER CONSTRUCT

We hold these truths of having
Been created equal tightly

In so doing, we remind ourselves in prayer
daily and nightly

Focus on goodness, self rely
Self sustain, **boldly** cry

Be true to who and how God made you stand

Educate where lessons come
Never hold out flattened palms
To beg
Instead rotate to shake a hand

(Your brothers hand)

Only look down
To tie your shoes and to teach young
Children who

Look up to you
As good women
And men

Seek favor only from above
Love all people. Receive love.
Again.

PLAYBOOK

If you win then what?

Then what

If you win then what?

You made a play
Then took a stand

Though how will vict'ry look?

Hold up a picture.
Share your plan

Your template
Your main diagram

Who's left standing in the end?
Who gave?
Who took?

Real Winners
follow
His instructions
Book.

YOUR MILE

I don't want to have to
wear your shoes.
Just to understand.

The torment you
have to endure
just to be a man.

Don't get me wrong.
I get you.
I have frustrations too.

It's my turn for the
breaks in life
They give to persons who.

Met he-he-oh criteria.
Checked the
'colored prospect' box.

Yeah years were same
for what's his name.
He'd had a few hard knocks.

Still cause contrite
It isn't right,
he got it over me.

Screw equal rights.
I lose. I'm White.
Darn this diversity!

BULL MARKET

Broad shoulders
and braids
Beckon
Big
Black Americans.
Bull;

Mark it.

But not seats in
Boardrooms
Bilateral
Buy
Booms
Or even big guys who
Can Pull...

At dreams of
Prosperity

Listen.
Wholeheartedly

All clear see
Surveillance
Ghosts - Boo!

Up to some good
Do tale this (you should)

Broad shoulders and
Braids want some too!

FURNITURE

Coffee table on all four legs just

upped and walked away.

The sofa slowly followed suit.

You had beans today

The television looks at you

It's very turned off. Sighs.

You too often change the channel

Based on who you're sitting by.

They're leaving.

You can stand and Tweet.

Entertain yourself by text

Keep treating them like objects,

People next

LAIRD

Absent owners.
Land sold to afar
Landlords are paid
To care

Highest bidders
Sign on bottom lines
Rootless of ruthless
Laird

Now haughty dreams
Mean nightmares
Fearing
Those in need

Unrecognized
Shaped Countrysides
Rambling Renters
Tumbleweed

Soil lives in
united states.
Owner ships
everywhere.

Piecemeal carve-out
scarred reveal
Sculptor sans
Deed declared

Homeless in homeland
Houseless
Some many;
Many broke

American Dream

So many done for profit.

aWoke (-J-)

-

HIGH NOON

I'll bring a rose to your gun fight

So we have to stand at close range

To see Eye to Eye

Hoping both can rely

On minds motives and

Moves making change.

Since I'm packing a rose,

please bring water

Since you're packing a gun,

I'll bring pleas

To stand foes-future-friends

Locked and loaded to end

Understanding the

Victor is

PEACE.

I LAYER

You deflect.
I layer.

Another coat of life

Dampened

The wayward splash

You dash.

You move away.

I layer.
Love back
Soak all of it in
Move much slower
Through the day

The deflection does not
Dissipate.

The strewn lands
Right here. See.

Close by

Completely covered in all
Deflected unto me

HERE

I do not want to leave here
Never existed
On your mind

I will dance in front of cameras
Leave impressions
Laugh. Unwind.

I will photo bomb the pictures
Of the tourists from afar
Though I don't drink or smoke at all
I'll hit a local bar

Introduce myself to patrons
Make sure they see me drinking
koke.

Take in the vibe.
Just be alive.
Laugh at corny jokes.

I'll take some random selfies
Pay for someone's parking time

When at the local grocery store
Let one ahead in line

Then go home and die.

THEY GO

They do not overdose

They go

So they are not here

And now, the hell

On earth that is

Stirring and

Feeding Fear

They escape for a

Moment

Or a lifetime or

The night

Until next

Destination Delivers Darkness
to the night
Or Light

MECHANISMS

Coping mechanisms are boundless

Laughter

Drawing

Dancing

Singing songs

Record them all to recall

It's ok if others sing along

Then play back

without soundtracks on

Just listen

Humor jewels will

shine through

and likely glisten

Or go paint a picture

with wet stuff

Or a pen

Or a pencil

Or a brush

Of some sort

Frame your favorite work

Your best mess message;

Maybe the one in making

Was most fun

Push substances aside

Take coping mechanism pride

Masterpiece

"Making Peace" no. 1

JIM, JACK AND STOLI

You, Jim, Jack and Stoli

Should not climb back inside that car

Put the keys down on the bar please

Since you won't get very far

Unless you're willing to risk killing,

Cars cannot climb up in trees

And little babies strapped in car seats

Can't bear the weight of SUVs.

So you, Jim, Jack and Stoli

Need to vote on what to do

Take the night to sleep it off

Or go hurt a child or two.

BORN

Beautiful priceless
Diamond
and the source from
whence it comes

Are both vital
In their own way
Both aware
Where they are from

The beauty outcomes
Shines through darkness
One will glisten
Source unseen

Creates pressure
Formed a jewel
Adored
For all eternity

THE PROBLEM

The problem is the problem
Not the people or the protests
Policemen or the pistols
there of

It's the problem that's the problem
Praise and pray for those who solve them
Guidance powers provide purpose from above

Point to mindset as the problem
Projected negatively solvent
The problem is the causer who

Blossom when they
Are part watered
By the dew of
bigger problems too

Prejudice promulgation
Pollution perpetuation
Profanity communication then

Weed out the problems
Leave the people
Propose solutions
Perceive needs for
Problem procreation to end

PALLIATIVE

Remove thorn from a lion's paw.

Hold a trembling hand.

Give a child a warm embrace.

Help them to understand.

The world is big and frightening.

We live until we die.

Sometimes we laugh til our

bellies ache.

Some aching makes us cry.

God promises us palliative love.

Embracing Him through pain.

Never alone en route to home

Until we dance again

YA KNOW

Can't say "ya know"
to anyone and they get
what I mean

No random calls from friends
From when
Everything all
Seemed...

All Great
All Happy
All good
All On top
And
All Fine

No worries
Good to go
Come in
Relax and unwind

In no hurry.
And in no rush
Are
Where
I long to go.

I really miss
Those days
Those people
I'm guessing
Yeah...
You know

BLUE

Staring in the mirror
I see my Daddy's
big Blue
Eyes

Twirling fingers
Through my curly locks
Mom's-me is no
Surprise

One in a
Million of the millions
Diverse DNAbled
Mod

Designed to Unite
Divide-ites
Personified
By God

WE POE

Me and Edgar Allan
Poe

Pour hearts out
in the words

Placed in our minds
So all can find

Inspiration heard

Me, Edger Allen,
Poe
Riches come from
prose

A wealth of verse
Exhumed, rehearsed
Poetry
Juxtaposed

Rewards?
They come in
Heaven
Countless artists
Know

Frugal fame
Fraternity
Me,
Edger Allen,
Po'

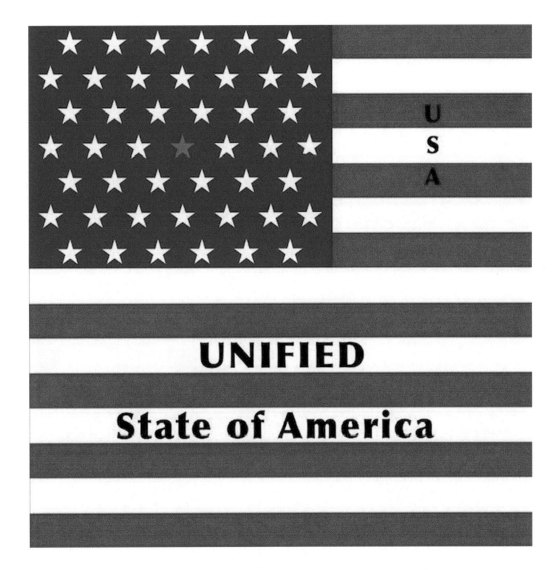

The Unified State of America art depiction was created by a middle school student. Context: Is peace moving backwards? Draw America of states united.

The flag is square; equal 4all sides. The 15 stripes represent the Voting Rights 15th Amendment. There are 51 stars. The 51st purple star represents Purple Heart Veterans. The color also symbolizes the bipartisan 'new unified' state of America and 51st state Washington, DC.

MASKING BLIND

The blind kid has no **vision**.

Bullying kids can't see

How wonderful he is inside;

the possibilities.

He tossed dark glasses,

ditched his cane

to look like others.

Find...

A friend or three

A place to be

No longer left behind.

Seeking...

Crossed divided road

no one saw he cried.

Friendless. Hopeless. Listless.

Now

Well, at least he tried.

SECOND BEST

Make them bigger better
Stronger
To last longer
Than the rest

Do not take away
Enhance it
Enrich power first
then test!

In our schools
YES
Educate all of inalienable rights

Of our citizens
Native, others from
Engaging foresight

With rights not to be
Stupid
Militia Rights to not be
Dumb

Add 1 word
"Educated"
Before
2nd Militia guns

Make a right to Education
Shoot straight STEM
All take the TEST

Build smarter human capital
No settling
'fer secund besst'

LOVE 4 COUNTRY CONFERENCE

Four years can seem like 44 marching around in wait
all are related. although belated it's never too late
For this resolution conference for us to finally see the

L.ove
O.rder
R.econciliation (moral)
D.iplomacy

Love of God and self and others
Order and a calm resolve
Reconciliation mindset
Diplomacy: true Moral one

Start at home to show alliance
World reliance happens next
Show our family blood is thicker
Share our **Unity** progress
Unity must be intention
if intend walk through the door

Progressed Success
past point of venting merely; nothing more
It's time for talking
Time for listening
Time for resolving
Time for real care

Weapons held but down.
unloaded.

what happens here is everywhere

and everyone.
All men. Again...
What's shot out here hits everywhere.

TRUE STORY

One day in summer 2021, we were traveling on the interstate in the carpool lane. That day all lanes except ours were flowing at normal speed. We moved at a snail's pace in contrast to the very purpose for all riding together. Dictated by no choice otherwise, we just stayed in our not-so-fast lane. Clearly something in the roadway was causing the slowdown. We feigned patience then adjusted temperaments accordingly. When the road blocking obstacle came into view, all better understood. We paid homage and gradually drove along through.

EAGLE PROCESSION

A bald eagle carcass lying against

Left concrete median

Reminded all those

in the fast lane

to slow down.

The fact that everyone did so

Somberly

Let everyone show

Respect

for our symbol still

Abounds.

Photo by Asher©

PENULTIMATE

Yesterday.

The last speech was the next to last time leaders had to say

Thoughts and prayers for the lives of service members lost today

When you make the promise keep it
So you will not have
Repeat it
Then relay

Condolences so kind
Folded flags, held do remind
Of the honor and the sacrifices made
So the next to last goodbye is
Not in vain.
Make the last goodbyes the ones we do

Today.

About the Author

J.S. Christian taught college English Rhetoric, Literature and Writing. A clear penchant is use of creative voice for justice. The Pepperdine Law alum pens poetic for conflict resolution advocacy in "...Advocate Poetically" (AP) books. Christian gives volume to those commonly silenced and uncommonly heralded. Their voices are immutable here. All willing to listen will hear through Christian's prose. Enjoy.

Printed in the United States
by Baker & Taylor Publisher Services